Table of Contents

Our Philosophy

The world is a smaller place these days, and children in our classrooms are from many cultures. This series offers stepping stones toward the goal of mutual respect among children of different backgrounds. The program offers an integrated curriculum, with whole class, cooperative group, and individual activities for the primary grades. Interviews were the primary source of information for the program, giving the hands-on activities their authenticity, detail, and interest.

A special thank you to Shoko Endo and Chizuko Mitsumoto for their invaluable contributions to this book.

Japan

Momotaro, the Peach Boy

Retold by Betsy Franco

Japanese Words in the Story:

Momotaro (Moh-moh´-tah-roh´) -- Peach Boy
Ohayo (Oh-hah´-yoh) -- Good morning
Kibi dumpling (kee-bee´) -- rice flour ball with sweetener
Onigashima (Oh-nee-gah´-shee-mah) -- Ogre's Island

2

Japan

In a small house by a stream lived a kindly old man and a loving old woman.

"We have a wonderful life," said the old woman, "but I wish we had a child of our own."

"Yes," said the old man who was repairing the thatched roof of their house, "That is my greatest wish, too."

Japan

That morning, the old woman was washing clothes in
the stream when a large, juicy peach came bobbing by.
She grabbed for it and brought it home for dinner.

The old man raised his knife to cut the peach in half
when suddenly a strange noise stopped him.
"Stretch...POP," was the sound as the peach burst open.
Out came a plump little boy with dark hair and sparkling
eyes.

"A boy of our own!" said the old woman with delight.
"We will name him Momotaro, the Peach Boy."

4

The old man and woman treasured their little boy, and he grew up to be very strong. Everything was wonderful, except for the ogres who lived nearby on an island called Onigashima. They came at night to steal and fight and cause trouble with the people who lived in the country.

When Momotaro was a boy of ten, he told the old man and the old woman, "I must make a journey to Onigashima to put a stop to the ogres."

The old people were frightened, but they helped him pack his bundle. He took a sword, the Japanese flag and the old woman's wonderful kibi dumplings.

Japan

The next morning Momotaro was on the road. He
had just gone over the steep temple bridge when he
saw a dandy dog resting beneath it.

"Ohayo, dog, how do you do?
I really need some help from you.
Please have a dumpling ball to chew,
Then come to Onigashima, too."

The dandy dog gobbled down the dumpling and joined
Momotaro the Peach Boy.

6   Japan

Just when they had gone through a grove of maple trees, they saw a merry monkey near the top of one of the trees...

"Ohayo, monkey, how do you do?
I really need some help from you.
Please have a dumpling ball to chew,
Then come to Onigashima, too."

The merry monkey leaped from the tree, gobbled down the dumpling, and joined the dandy dog and Momotaro the Peach Boy.

Japan

After crossing a stream, the band of followers
heard a friendly pheasant singing above them.

"Ohayo, pheasant, how do you do?
I really need some help from you.
Please have a dumpling ball to chew,
Then come to Onigashima, too."

The friendly pheasant was happy to join the dandy dog,
the merry monkey and Momotaro the Peach Boy.

8   Japan

They finally reached the beach where they
took a boat to Onigashima, the Island of Ogres.
Momotaro gave the pheasant instructions, "Go tell
the chief of the ogres that I have come."

 Japan

The pheasant flew off to give his message.
Then the crew sailed to the island. Quickly, the
pheasant flew up and unlatched the gates, and the
monkey scrambled over the wall. The dog and
Momotaro began fighting the ogres. Blue, red and
green they were, with terrible screeching voices and
ugly faces.

10   Japan

The pheasant pecked at their heads, the
monkey jumped on their backs, the dog bit their
heels, and Momotaro used his mighty sword.

Finally, Momotaro found their chief. With a
loud cry, he pinned the red ogre to the ground.
"Look at your chief now," he cried.

The other cowardly ogres were frightened.
They begged for mercy and offered treasures to
Momotaro.

                                            Japan

With a cart full of treasures, Momotaro
returned home. The friendly pheasant flew above
the treasures. The merry monkey pushed the cart.
And the dandy dog pulled the cart.

Momotaro the Peach Boy carried the flag of
Japan and was a hero for defeating the terrible
ogres of Onigashima.

 Japan

Folktale Follow-Up

1. What do you notice about the way the characters are dressed?

The old woman and the old man are dressed in kimonos. The straw "sandals" the people are wearing are called zori. Momotaro is wearing the outfit of a Samurai, a warrior in old Japan.

For special occasions, people in Japan still wear kimonos. Some older people wear kimonos every day.

2. Tell some things you learned about a Japanese house.

When you enter a Japanese home today, you take off your shoes. Paper slippers or regular slippers are often provided. The floor in Momotaro's house is covered by tatami mats made of straw, which are still found in many Japanese homes. Some Japanese sleep on futon, or sleeping mats, that can be put in a closet during the day.

3. Tell what you learned about Japanese food.

The food that Momotaro ate consisted of wheat with a sweetener added and formed into a ball. Rice is the main staple of the Japanese diet.

4. What Japanese words did you hear in the story?

ohayo -- good morning

kibi dumpling -- rice flour dumpling

Onigashima -- Ogre's Island

5. What do you think the flag of Japan represents?

The flag represents the rising sun.

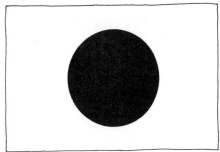

 Japan

Other ways to use *Momotaro, the Peach Boy*

• Reproduce the story several times. Staple each copy inside a cover. Send the copies home with different children each night until all students have had an opportunity to share the story with their families. You may want parents to write a comment on the back cover explaining how their family shared the book and how they felt about it.

• If your students are at a level where they can read the story themselves, reproduce several copies for children to use for shared reading.

• Once your students are familiar with the story, reproduce the pictures on page 15. Have children cut the pictures apart and put them in the sequence they occur in the story. The pictures can then be used to...

1. Paste to a large sheet of paper in the correct order.

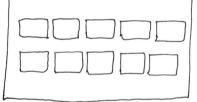

2. Create a picture book.
   • Paste the pictures into a book.
   • Use the pictures as you retell the story to a friend.

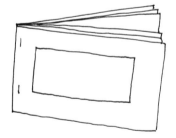

3. Rewrite the story.
   • Paste each picture to a sheet of writing paper.
   • Write about that part of the story.
   • Staple the finished pages together in order.
   • Make a cover for your book.

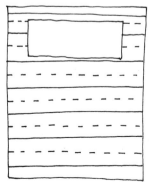

Note: Reproduce to use in retelling the story of **Momotaro, the Peach Boy.**

Pocket Chart Activity

Cut out the strips on pages 17-19 and place them in a pocket chart.

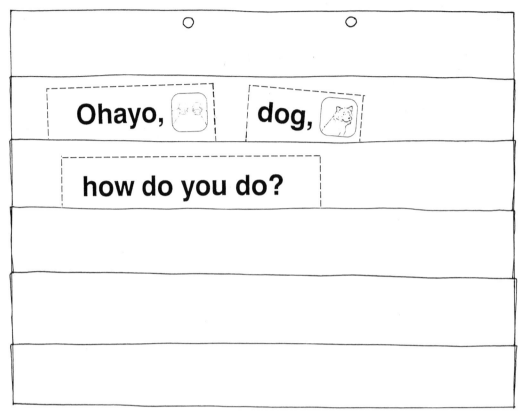

The chant can be read over and over again:

• It can be read after the first reading of the folktale and chanted over and over again, inserting the name of each animal. Then in the second reading of the folktale, the children can join in on the verses.

• It can be read prior to the folktale.

Below are some suggestions for this particular chant:

• Have the children tell what kind of a voice Momotaro probably used -- mean, friendly, loud or soft? Let the children try chanting in different ways.

• Ask the children which one word changes as the story progresses (the name of the animal).

• Have the children explore the rhyming words at the end of each line. Let them discover that they all rhyme.

• Point out the question mark. Ask how it changes the sentence.

Pocket Chart Strips

monkey,

dog,

Ohayo,

pheasant,

how do you do?

I really need some help from you.

Then come to Onigashima, too.

Please have a dumpling ball to chew,

19

Japan

Momotaro's
Story Mat

Japan

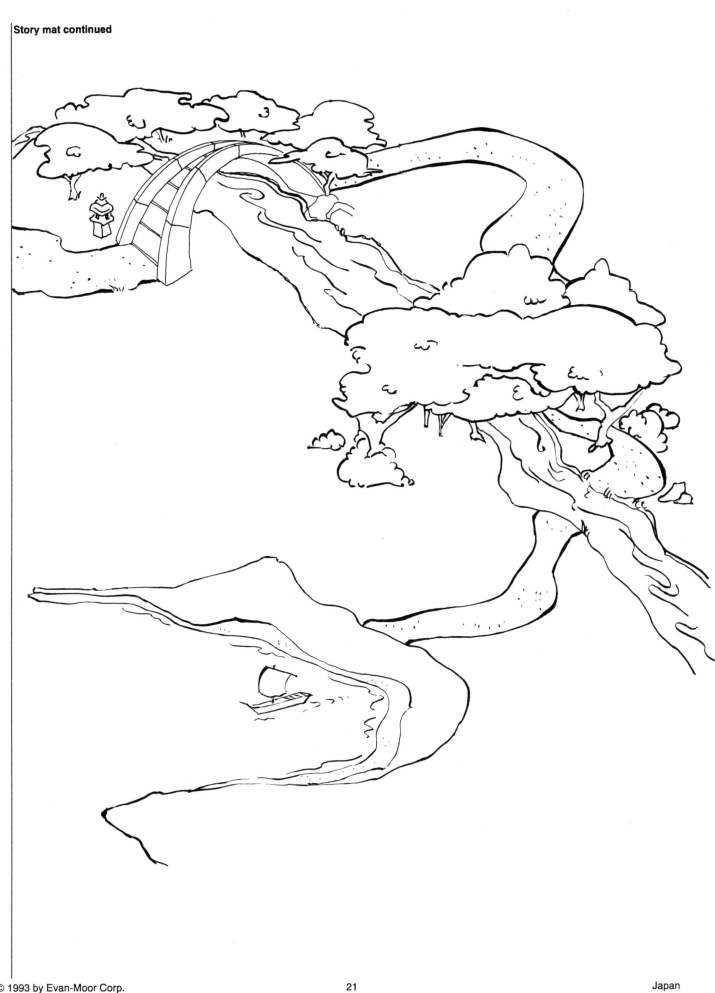

Japan

Characters

Use the characters on the Story Mat to act out the folktale **Momotaro, the Peach Boy** as your teacher reads it. You may act out the story in small groups.

1. Color in
2. Cut out
3. Fold
4. Glue

fold   fold   fold

paste   paste

paste   paste

paste   paste

paste   paste

paste   paste

22   Japan

Japanese "Picture Words"
Writing a Story

Cultural background

The Japanese written language includes pictures that stand for words. These ancient characters are called Kanji (kahn'-jee) characters. Originally from China, the characters look like those in Chinese, but the pronunciation is different. Some of the kanji look remarkably like the words they represent:

Preparation

- Reproduce pages 24 and 25 to use as a chart to display in the classroom.
- Each small group will need:
    1. several copies of the picture word card forms on page 26
    2. glue and scissors
    3. chart paper

Japanese "Picture Words"

child 子	horse 馬
river 川	person 人
fire 火	mountain 山
rain 雨	forest 森

Activity

- Display the large Japanese written characters. Cover the English words and see if your children can guess their meanings. You might need to give hints.

- *Pre-writers* - Divide the children into small groups, and pass out the picture word cards on page 26. Help the children create a story using these words. Let each child contribute a sentence or two. As they compose, you can transcribe the story onto chart paper, letting the children glue on each picture word where it appears in the story.

- *Writers* - Children can do the same activity in pairs. Emphasize that partners should take turns creating the story and gluing the picture words.

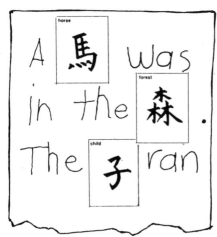

23   Japan

Japanese "Picture Words"

child

horse

river

person

 Japan

fire

mountain

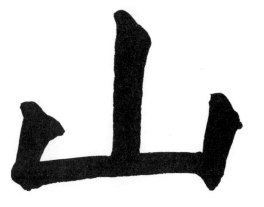

rain

forest

Japan

fire	fire	mountain	mountain
火	火	山	山
rain	rain	forest	forest
雨	雨	森	森
child	child	horse	horse
子	子	馬	馬
river	river	person	person
川	川	人	人

Japan

Playing a Board Game
Gomoku (Goh-moh´-koo)

Cultural Background

In the name Gomoku, Go means "five" and moku means "intersections." This board game for two players is an ancient game that is popular among young children in Japan. It is played on grid paper or on a board, which can also be used for the famous game of "Go."

Preparation

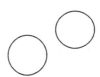

For each pair:

> • 1 piece of graph paper or the form on page 28

> • 2 pencils to draw the game moves (or beads of 2 different colors)

Activity

• Demonstrate for children how to play the game:

> One child is the light circle O and the other is the dark circle ● (Beads can be used as well).
>
> Children take turns filling in an intersection of the grid using their circle.
>
> The point is to be the first to make five circles in a row -- horizontally, vertically, or diagonally.

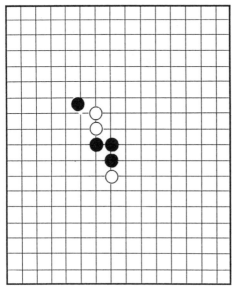

• Divide the children into pairs. Give each a grid and pencils (or beads) with which to play the game.

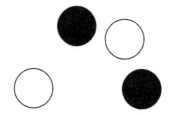

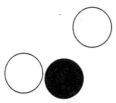

Japan

Gomoku

five in a row

Japan

Celebrating Tanabata
The Star Festival

Cultural Background

On the seventh day of the seventh month, the Japanese celebrate the Star Festival, Tanabata (Tah-nah´-bah-tah). They make origami figures to hang on a bamboo branch. They write wishes on strips of paper to hang on the branch as well. This celebration is based on a legend about two stars, Vega the Weaver Star and Altair the Cowherd Star. These stars were said to meet each other only once a year on July 7.

Preparation

Find a large tree branch. Hang it up or display it on a table or counter.

For each child:

- a piece of origami paper cut in half
  (You can use colored copy paper.)
- a strip of paper 6 to 8 inches (15 x 20.5 cm)
  long, with a hole punched in one end
  and a string tied through the hole.

Activity: Making Origami Decorations

Here is a traditional decoration for hanging on the tree branch:

Fold the paper
and cut along
the lines.

These decorations can also be made and hung:

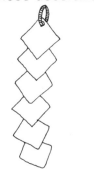

small squares
pasted together

strips of colored paper
glued and linked

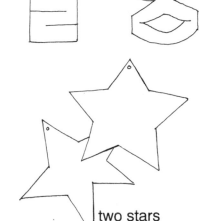

two stars

Japan

Writing a Wish

• Use this reproducible form to help children write wish poems.

I wish _____

I wish _____

I wish _____

and I wish _____

⬯ punch hole

I wish _____

I wish _____

I wish _____

and I wish _____

⬯ punch hole

• Remind them that wishes can be wild, impossible, make-believe, or real.

• Help them rewrite their favorite wish onto a slip of paper to hang on the tree branch.

Singing Japanese Songs

Cultural Background

The song below is sung throughout Japan by primary children. Everyone knows it. The song is written in romanized Japanese. The translation is as follows:

Springtime came. Springtime came.
Where did it come?
It came in the mountains.
It came in the village.
It also came in the fields.

Preparation

You might want to become familiar with the pronunciation and the melody of the song. It has a simple tune.

Activity

Ha - ru ga ki - ta ha - ru ga ki - ta Do - ko ni ki - ta --   ya - ma ni ki - ta.

Sa - to ni ki - ta. No - ni mo ki - ta.

Pronunciation			
Hah´-roo ga	kee-tah´	hah´-roo ga	kee-tah´
Doh´-koh	nee	kee-tah´	
Yah-mah´	nee	kee-tah´.	
Sah-toh´	nee	kee-tah´.	
Noh-nee´	moh	kee-tah´.	

   Japan

Practicing on a Soroban
(Soh-roh'-bahn)

Cultural Background
Children in Japan learn to use the soroban starting in third grade. Each bead on the top is worth 5 and each bead on the bottom is worth 1. The first column is ones. The second column is tens, the third is hundreds and so on. To create a number on the soroban, you push beads towards the cross bar. Thus the soroban below shows 78. The soroban is like an early calculator. You can add, subtract, multiply and divide. Even to this day, some shopkeepers in Japan use the soroban to add up a purchase.

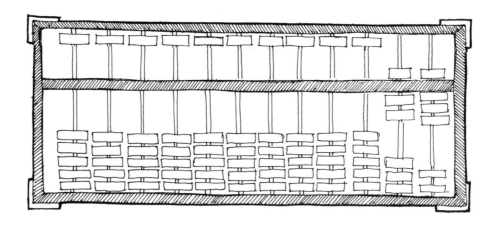

Preparation

For each child:
• ball of clay
• 3 bamboo shish kebob
  skewers (cut off sharp points)
• 25 Cheerios

For each pair:
• a die

Activity 1: Make a simple place value tool.
Have children use clay to form a base for their place value tool. Poke the skewers into the clay in a uniform row.

Tell them the first skewer on the right holds the <u>ones.</u>
The next holds the <u>tens.</u>
Ask what the third column must be.

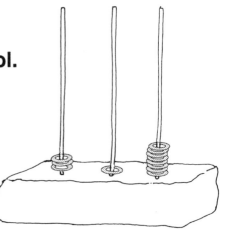

Japan

Activity 2: Practice place value

Pair the children up so they can help each other.
Guide the exploration with the whole group:

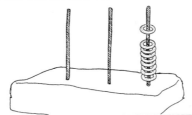

Teacher: Place 8 Cheerios on the *ones* stick.
Comments: Be sure the children know which is the "ones" column.

Teacher: Put on one more Cheerio. How many do you have now?

Teacher: Put on one more Cheerio. How many do you have?
Does anyone have a suggestion about trading in these 10 Cheerios?
Comments: Let children discover that 10 "ones" is 1 "ten."

Teacher: Add on 7 more to the "ones" column.
What number have we made?
Add on 4 more.
What do we do now?
Comments: Solicit ideas about how to trade. Let children devise their own methods for trading.

Teacher: Clear your "place value tool."
Put on 9 "tens" or 90.
Put on one more "ten." What can we do now?
Comments: Let children discover that 10 "tens" is 1 "hundred."

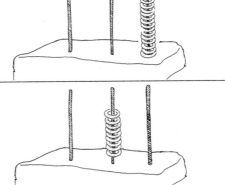

Activity 3: Play Game: "First to Fifty"

• Have pairs of children play a game using a die and their place value sticks and Cheerios.
• Children take turns rolling the dice to determine how many Cheerios to put on their sticks.
• The first one to reach 50 wins.

     Japan

Writing Haiku
(hah-ee´-koo)

Cultural Background

Haiku is the shortest form of poetry in Japan. Traditionally, it is three lines, with a total of seventeen syllables -- 5 syllables in the first line, 7 in the second, and 5 in the third. It does not rhyme. The subject matter of haiku is the little things you see, hear, taste, smell and feel, particularly in nature. Ancient haiku usually had a seasonal clue in it as well: frog = early summer, cricket = fall, heavy snow = winter, butterfly = spring. Here are two haiku by Basho, a famous Japanese poet. (In Japanese, these follow a 5-7-5 syllable pattern).

A quiet old pond --

In jumps a frog.

The sound of the splash!

Wake up. Wake up.

Let's be friends,

Sleeping butterfly.

Preparation

For each child, on the walk:
• paper and pencil for drawing and writing
• clipboard or something hard on which to write

For each child, for making a "scroll":
• construction paper
• glue
• 2 pieces of white paper (4" x 6" - 10 x 15 cm)(1 for poem, 1 for illustration)
• string

You will also need a stapler.

Japan

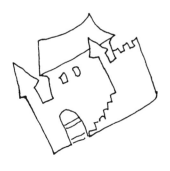

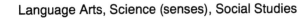

The large sand castle that we built the day before has been washed away.

Activity

• Talk about traditional haiku subjects (nature, seasons, small incidents) and form (5-7-5 syllables). Clap out the following 5-7-5 haiku together:

• Explain that nowadays the rules about writing haiku are not so strict. They can be three lines of any length (not just 5-7-5) or just one line.

• Go for a "Haiku Walk." Ask the children to bring a paper, pencil and something hard on which to write. Let the children point out small things that are special or interesting -- a flower just beginning to open, the shadow of grass along the sidewalk, an ant climbing a tree, the sound of a dog barking.

• Let each child take a few minutes to sit down in a special place to write and/ or draw something they liked on the walk or something they notice while sitting still. Remind them that it could be a sight, sound, smell, texture, or feeling.

• *Pre-writers* Back in the classroom: let the children dictate a haiku description of their drawing and make a colored picture on the pre-cut white papers.

   Writers Back in the classroom: let them finalize their haiku and their drawings on the pre-cut white papers.

• Let children finalize their scrolls by gluing the haiku and the illustration onto construction paper. Help them roll over the top, staple it, and tie a string through the opening.

Make an Origami Samurai

Cultural Background

Origami means folded (ori) paper (gami). It started about one thousand years ago. At that time, paper was so expensive that only a few people folded paper and only for serious ceremonies. Later it became a craft that mothers and grandmothers passed on to their children and grandchildren. The origami figure you will be making is a Samurai, a warrior of old Japan. Momotaro is a Samurai in the folktale.

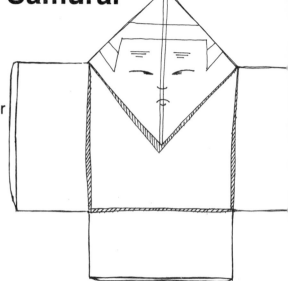

Preparation

For each child, to make the Samurai:
• 1 piece of origami or photocopy paper about 6" x 6" (15 x 15 cm)
• felt pens

For each child, to create a story scene:
• glue
• felt pens
• white paper

Activity

• Have children meet in small groups. Assign partners so children can help each other.
• You may want to demonstrate the following directions with a large piece of paper. (Folding wax paper on an overhead also works.) As you complete each step, help children spot the geometric shapes they are creating.
• Have students complete the folding steps to make the samurai. They can use felt pens to add details.
• Have the children glue their origami samurai onto the white paper. They complete the picture by illustrating a scene from **Momotaro, the Peach Boy**.

Japan

Folding Steps:

Step 1

Lay your paper flat on the table. What shape is your paper? (square).

How do you know it's a square? (All sides same length)

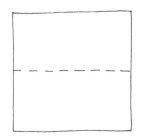

Step 2

Fold your paper in half. What shape do you see now? (rectangle)

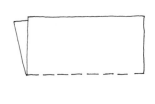

Step 3

Fold your paper in half the other way. What shape do you have? (square)

Step 4

Open up your paper. How many shapes do you see? (4)

How are they the same? (all square, all same size)

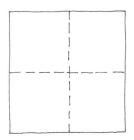

Step 5

Fold one corner to the center. What shape have you made? (triangle)

Now fold all the other corners to the center.

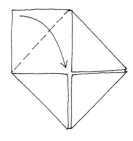

Step 6

Turn your paper over and fold all corners to the center. How do you know all the triangles are the same size and shape? (Can fold them onto each other.)

Step 7

Turn your paper over and fold all the corners to the center.

Step 8

Turn your paper over again. Put your finger under one of the small squares and push it outward.

Then squash it down. What shape have you made? (rectangle)

Step 9

Repeat step 8 with two more small squares. You have made Momotaro! The square is his head and the rest is his Samurai outfit.

Japan

Playing a Team Game
Jan Ken Pon (Jahn Kehn Pohn)

Cultural Background
This game played in elementary school throughout Japan is like the game "Rock-Paper-Scissors." Japanese children say, "Jan-Ken-Pon" instead of "Rock, Paper, Scissors."

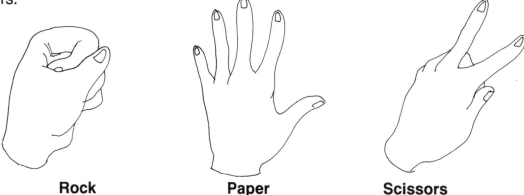

Rock   **Paper**   **Scissors**

Paper covers rock; rock breaks scissors; scissors cut paper

Preparation
Children will probably need to play this game outside because of the speed of the game and the need to run back and forth.

Activity
• Divide the children into teams of 5 or 6. Line them up as shown below:

A B C D E

F G H I J

• **E** and **F** run and meet in the middle, and they do "Jan-Ken-Pon." Whoever loses runs to the end of his/her line quickly. Whoever wins plays the next player on the opposite team and keeps going until he/she loses (e.g., if **E** beats **F**, then **E** and **G** would play next).

• If one player makes it through everyone on the other team, that player's team wins the game.

• The game is played very quickly with lots of running as children meet each other in the middle and return to the end of the line.

                   Japan

How to Use the Counting Chart

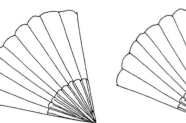 

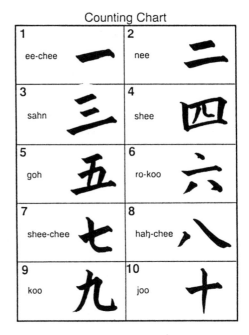

Counting Chart	
1 ee-chee 一	2 nee 二
3 sahn 三	4 shee 四
5 goh 五	6 ro-koo 六
7 shee-chee 七	8 haḥ-chee 八
9 koo 九	10 joo 十

Use the Counting Chart on page 40 to acquaint children with how the Japanese count to ten. Leave the chart up in the classroom for the students to refer to while you are doing this unit on Japan.

1. Provide students with many opportunities to count in Japanese. Let them count chopsticks, beads on the soroban, etc.

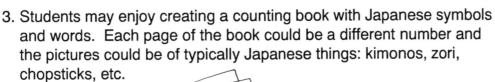

2. Allow students a chance to go to a paint center and practice writing the Japanese symbols for the number.

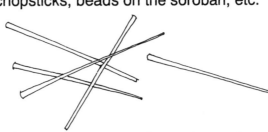

3. Students may enjoy creating a counting book with Japanese symbols and words. Each page of the book could be a different number and the pictures could be of typically Japanese things: kimonos, zori, chopsticks, etc.

4. Make a copy of the Counting Chart. Cut the numbers apart and let the students sequence the numerals as they count.

Counting Chart

1 ee-chee 一	**2** nee 二
3 sahn 三	**4** shee 四
5 goh 五	**6** ro-koo 六
7 shee-chee 七	**8** hah-chee 八
9 koo 九	**10** joo 十

How to Make a Fish Kite

May 5 is Children's Day in Japan. It was once celebrated as Tango no Sekku (Boy's Festival). A kite in the shape of a carp was flown outside the house for each boy in the family. The carp represents qualities parents want their children to posses... strength, courage and determination.

Preparation

Each child will need:

- Tagboard strips - 1" X 12" (2.5 X 30.5 cm)
- Material for fish - butcher paper, tissue paper or unbleached muslin for this project.
    - 12" X 20" (30.5 X 50.7 cm) - 1 per child
    - 2"X 8" (5.0 X 20.5 cm) - 2 per child
    - 2" X 12" (5.0 X 30.5 cm) - 6 per child
- Crayons or felt pens
- Glue
- Scissors
- Hole punch
- String
- Stick - 1 per child - This can be dowling, bamboo plant stakes, or thin branches

Steps to follow:

1. Form a ring by stapling the tag strip.

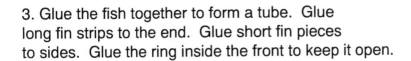

2. Decorate your material with eyes, gills, scales using crayons or marking pens. If paper, draw your designs. If cloth, draw your design with wax crayon, cover with newspaper and press with a warm iron to set the color. (Teacher needs to do this for younger students.)

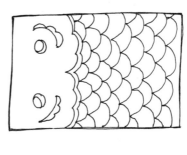

3. Glue the fish together to form a tube. Glue long fin strips to the end. Glue short fin pieces to sides. Glue the ring inside the front to keep it open.

4. Make three holes in the ring end with a hole punch. Tie 15" strings to each hole. Tie the other end to your stick.

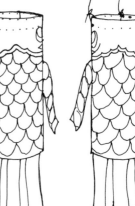

5. Make three holes in the ring end with a hole punch. Tie 15" (38.5 cm) strings to each hole. Tie the other end of each string to your stick.

Take outside - run across playground to make the fish "swim" in the air.

Japan

Note: How about reading *How My Parents Learned to Eat* as your children practice using chopsticks.

How to Eat with Chopsticks

Provide each child with a pair of chopsticks. (You can often buy cheap sets at the grocery store. If not, make friends with your local Japanese or Chinese restaurant.)

Help them follow these steps to pick up food with chopsticks.

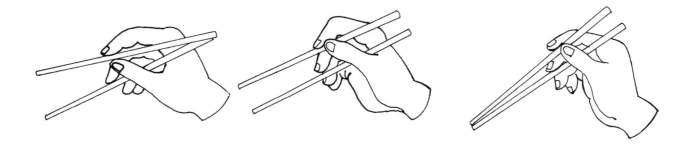

Small balls of rice are good for practicing using chopsticks. Cook a large batch of rice (gummy rice will work best). If you cook the rice at school with your students, be sure to let it cool before beginning the next step. Give each child a paper plate with rice. Have them make their own rice balls by squeezing together bits of rice. This would be a fun time to practice counting in Japanese. (See page 43.) Children could count each rice ball as they make it. When everyone has completed their rice balls, let them experiment with using the chopsticks. Remind them that this is not easy for children who have always used forks and spoons. Expect a lot of spills and giggles.

Japan

Obento
box lunch for primary students

onigiri - rice ball with seaweed and some seasonings

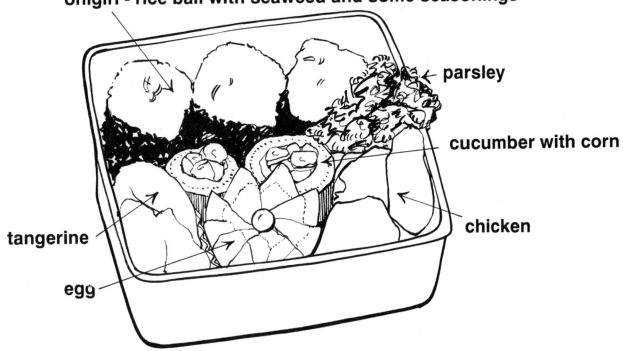

parsley

cucumber with corn

chicken

tangerine

egg

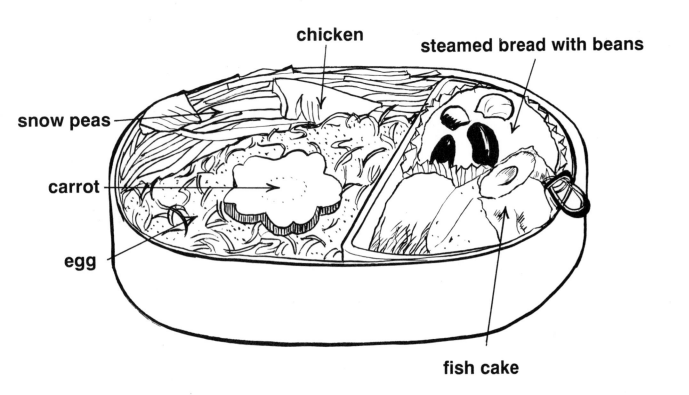

chicken

steamed bread with beans

snow peas

carrot

egg

fish cake

March 3 - Hina Matsuri

Here is a picture of a charming Japanese doll. Dolls are important to children for play, but they also are a part of a special festival.

Hina Matsuri is an ancient festival. It has changed over the years. Nowadays, girls display special dolls on stands covered with red cloth.

The dolls represent the members of a royal court. There can be as many as 15 dolls representing a emperor, his wife and their attendants. These special dolls are sometimes handed down from mother to daughter.

On March 3, girls visit each other to see the doll displays. They may also serve refreshments in honor of the special occasion.

Japan

Children in Japan dress in many ways. Most, like the children below, wear uniforms to school. For festivals and celebrations, children might dress in special clothing. The rest of the time, boys and girls in Japan dress in the same kinds of clothing you might be wearing.

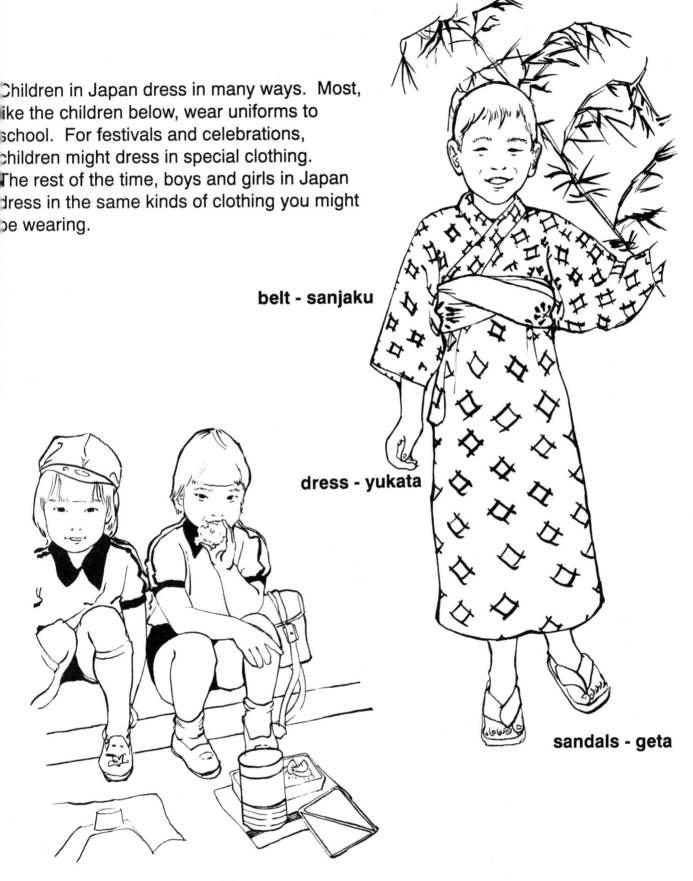

belt - sanjaku

dress - yukata

sandals - geta

school uniform

Flag of Japan

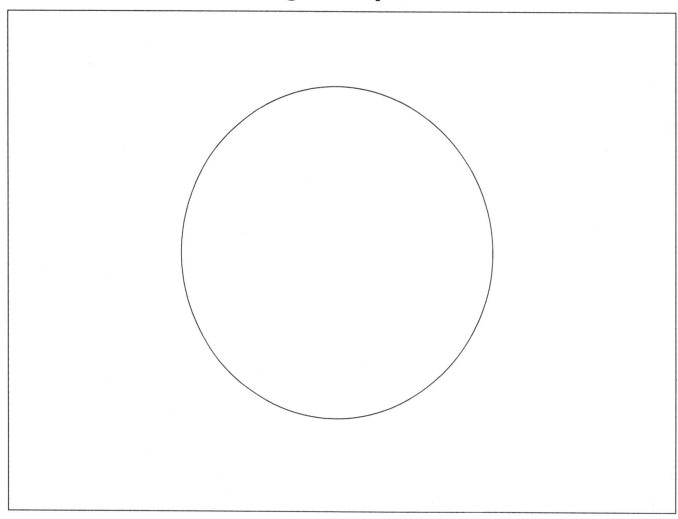

This is the flag of Japan.
It is white and red.
The red center stands for the sun.
Japan is sometimes called "Land of the Rising Sun."

Japan is a country of many islands.
It has four main islands.
It has many high mountains.
It has rivers and lakes.

Japan has many large cities.
Many people live in these cities.
Tokyo is the capital city of Japan.
Many things you use come from Japan.

Japan

Map of Japan

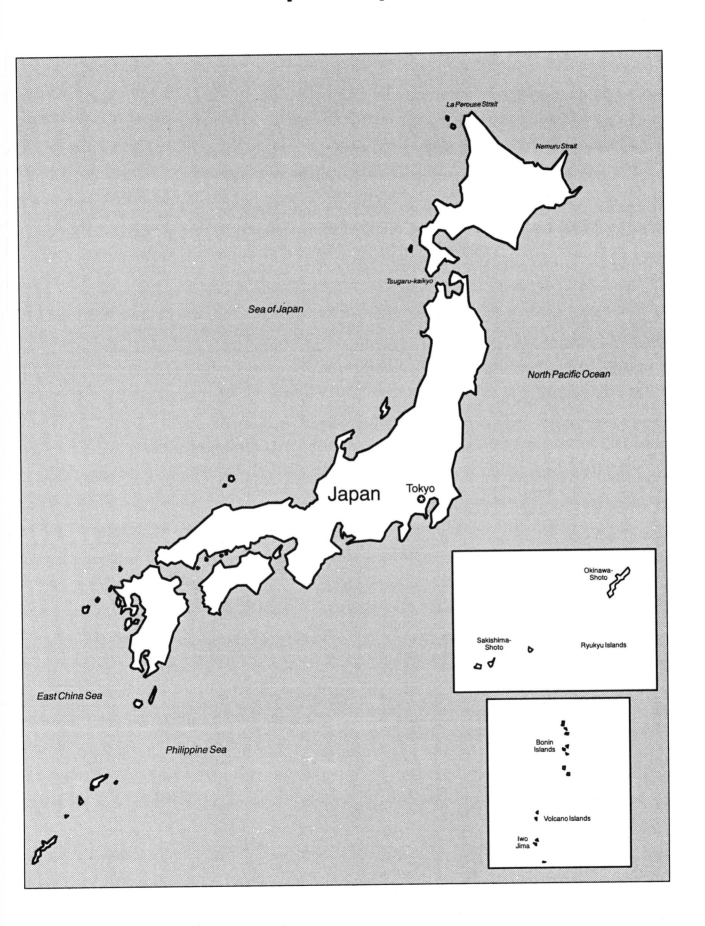

La Perouse Strait

Nemuru Strait

Tsugaru-kaikyo

Sea of Japan

North Pacific Ocean

Japan

Tokyo

East China Sea

Philippine Sea

Okinawa-Shoto

Sakishima-Shoto

Ryukyu Islands

Bonin Islands

Volcano Islands

Iwo Jima

Japan

Glossary

ame (ah´-may) rain

Basho (Bah-shoh´) Japanese poet who wrote Haiku

futon (foo-tahn´) sleeping mat that can be put away during the day

Gomoku (Goh-moh'-koo) children's game; go means "five;" moku means "intersections"

Haiku (Hah-ee´-koo) shortest poetry form in Japan

haru (hah´-roo) spring

Jan Ken Pon (Jahn Kehn Pohn) children's game like "Rock-Paper-Scissors"

Kanji (Kahn´-jee) Japanese picture words; derived from Chinese characters, with different pronunciation

kibi dumpling (kee-bee´) type of dumplingin Japan, consisting of a steamed rice flour ball rolled in sweetener

kimono (kee-moh´-noh) traditional form of dress

Momotaro (Moh-moh´-tah-roh) Peach Boy

ohayo (oh-hah´-yoh) short form of "good morning"

Onigashima (Oh-nee-gah´-shee-mah) Ogre's Island

origami (oh-ree´-gah-mee) the art of paper folding

Samurai (Sah-moo´-rah-ee) warrior of old Japan

soroban (soh-roh´-bahn) Japanese abacus

Tanabata (Tah-nah´-bah-tah) Star Festival

tatami (tah-tah´-mee) straw floor covering

zori (zoh´-ree) sandal-type shoe made of rice straw

e as in feed	ee
e as in bed	eh
o as in wrote	oh
o as in cot	ah
u as in flute	oo

Japan